Microsoft Dynamics 365 Quality Management

A complete review of the essential setups needed to implement D365 QC

Andrew F. Weber

ISBN: 9781792779183

Table of Contents

Introduction

This is a D365 QC module essentials handbook. All basic and requisite setups, with typical transaction examples, are included. The document assumes knowledge of the following:

Item and bom setup

Production Order administration

PO administration and processes

Sales Order administration and processes

No advanced warehousing setups are used in the examples. Serial and Batch tracking options are not covered in this document.

Setup explanations and field input recommendations precede each screen copy. Data inputs and nomenclature can be found on the screen copies. If a field is not mentioned, it is not needed for that setup example. The table of contents is also a setup sequence summary.

About the Author: Andrew Weber is a certified AX and D365 developer and implementer. He can be reached at AndrewFWeber@gmail.com

Product version: Microsoft Dynamics 365 for Finance and Operations (8.0)

Platform version: Update 15

<u>SETUP</u>

<u>MENUS</u>

Note: Instructions precede screen copies

1. Open the Inventory Management module

    1. 'Periodic tasks > Quality Management' provides forms to administer quality management types

    2. 'Setup > Quality Control' primarily relates to Quality Orders

    3. 'Setup > Quality Management' relates primarily to Non-conformances

▷ Workspaces

◢ Modules

   Accounts payable

   Accounts receivable

   Audit workbench

   Budgeting

   Cash and bank management

   Common

   Consolidations

   Cost accounting

   Cost management

   Credit and collections

   Demo data

   Expense management

   Fixed assets

   Fleet management

   General ledger

   Human resources

   Inventory management

   Master planning

   Organization administration

   Payroll

   Procurement and sourcing

   Product information management

   Production control

   Project management and accounting

   Questionnaire

   Retail

   Sales and marketing

   Service management

▷ Inbound orders

▷ Outbound orders

▷ Journal entries

◢ Inquiries and reports

   On-hand list

   Counting history

   Operations infrastructure

  ▷ Tracking dimensions

◢ Quality management

   Certificate of analysis

   Related operation items

   Related operation charges

   Related operation time sheets

   Non conformance

   Non conformance tag

   Corrections

▷ Transfer orders

▷ Batches

▷ Packing material reports

▷ Location reports

▷ Transactional reports

▷ On-hand reports

▷ Physical inventory reports

▷ Inventory value reports

◢ Periodic tasks

   Closing and adjustment

   Planned transfer orders

   Release sales order picking

   Release transfer order picking

   Picking workbench

   Inventory blocking

   ABC classification

   Linked dimension update

   Schedule load utilization

   Schedule workload

  ▷ Transfer update

  ▷ Bills of materials

  ◢ Quality management

    Quarantine orders

    Quality orders

    Non conformances

    Corrections

  ▷ Locations

  ▷ Clean up

  ▷ Commodity pricing

  ▷ Batches

  ▷ Forecast updates

◢ Setup

   Inventory and warehouse management parameters

▷ Price/discount

▷ Charges

▷ Supplementary items

▷ Distribution

▷ Inventory

▷ Inventory breakdown

▷ Warehouse monitoring

▷ Bills of materials

◢ Quality control

   Test instruments

   Tests

   Test variables

   Test groups

   Quality associations

   Quality groups

   Item quality groups

   Item sampling

   Workers responsible for quality

◢ Quality management

   Diagnostic types

   Quality charges

   Operations

   Problem types

   Quarantine zones

▷ Journal names

2. Production Order action tab sub-section

3. Purchase Order action tab sub-section

4. Sales Order action tab sub-section

Inventory and Whse Management

Parameters, Quality Management

Note: Instructions precede screen copies

1. Click the Use Quality Management flag to Yes

2. Hourly Rate is used to provide a reference and calculate cost for labor on non-conformances (optional)

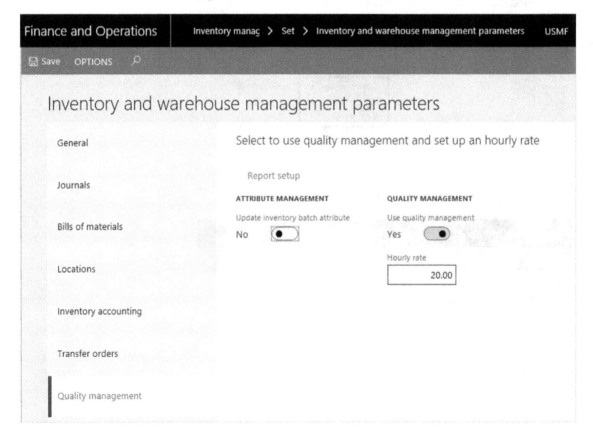

3. Click the blue Report Setup tab to open the Report Setup form

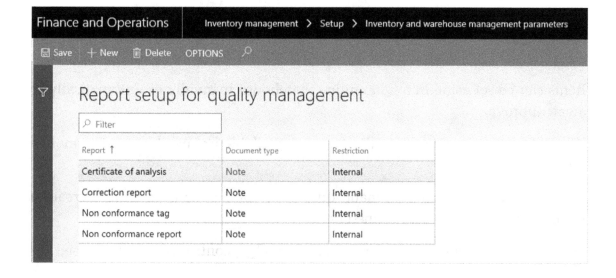

<u>Quarantine Warehouse</u>

Note: Instructions precede screen copies

Items can be set aside in a Quarantine warehouse manually or automatically to await approval.

When items are in quarantine they are not available in inventory and cannot be picked for delivery.

To enable a manual or automatic quarantine of an item, you must create a warehouse to hold the quarantined item.

Quarantine Warehouse items are in effect **quality** controlled, until released for use.

1.　Create Quarantine Warehouse

2.　Note that the Quarantine Warehouse is subsequently applied against warehouse type 'default'

　　1.　If an item to be quarantined is stored in a warehouse that has no Quarantine warehouse linked to it, D365 stops updating and provides an error message that no quarantine warehouse was specified.

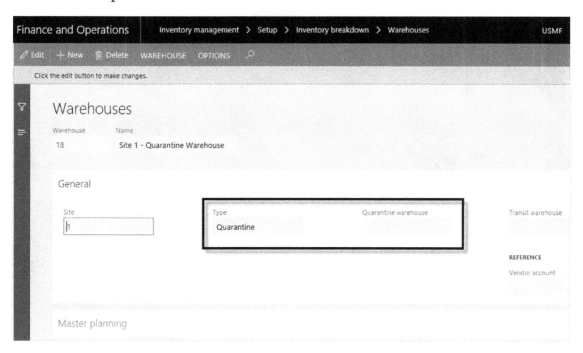

Quarantine Management

Note: Instructions precede screen copies

1. Automated Quarantine Management is enabled via Item Model Groups

    1. If not enabled, Quarantine Orders can be created manually

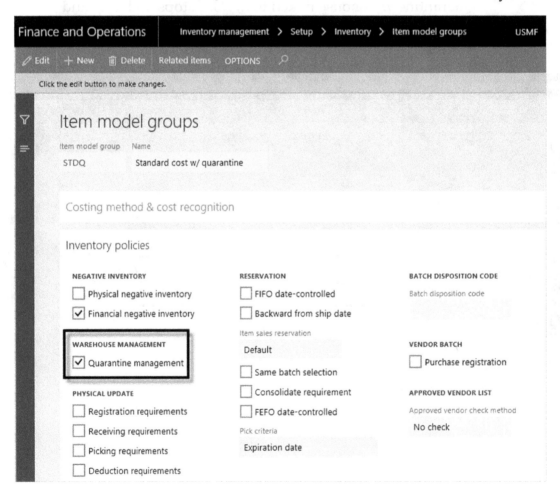

2. Assign Item Model Group to the part.

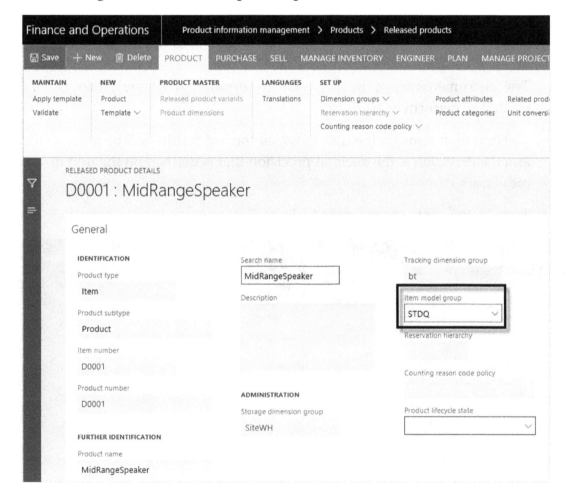

Test Instruments

Note: Instructions precede screen copies

1. Test instruments are optionally used to determine what equipment is needed to perform a test.

2. The unit of measure is the unit in which the test results will be measured, and the precision is the decimal precision that is defined on the unit of measure.

3. Tests Instruments are assigned to Tests

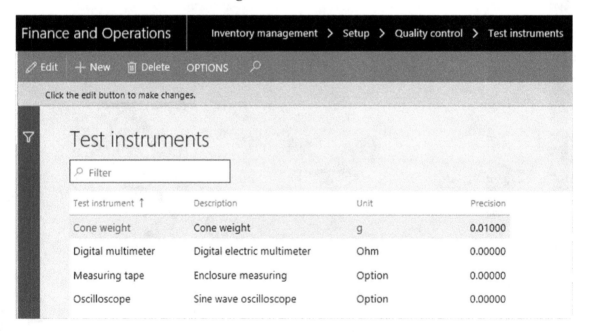

Tests

Note: Instructions precede screen copies

1. The test defines what action the worker performs. This is a mandatory setup. Three test measurement types can be defined in the type field:

    1. A quantitative tests is defined as type Integer or Fraction, and also has a unit of measure. Test results are recorded as numbers.

    2. A qualitative test is defined as type Option. Quality specifications and test results are recorded according to outcomes.

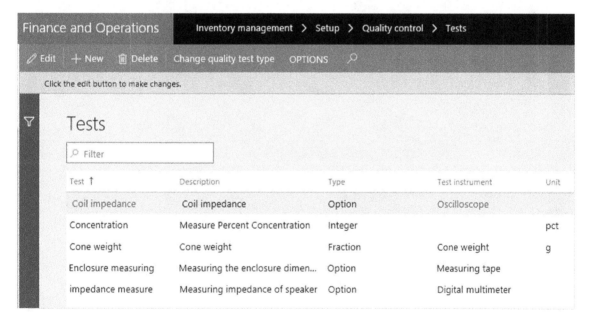

Test Variables

Note: Instructions precede screen copies

1.   Test variables are linked to Tests that are defined with the type Option <u>via</u> <u>Test Groups</u> using an outcome of Pass or Fail.

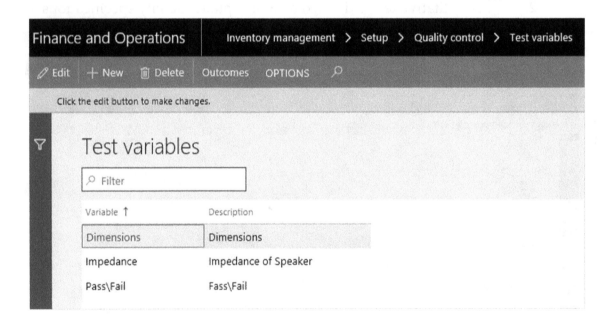

2.   Click Outcomes button at top of form to define pass/fail options

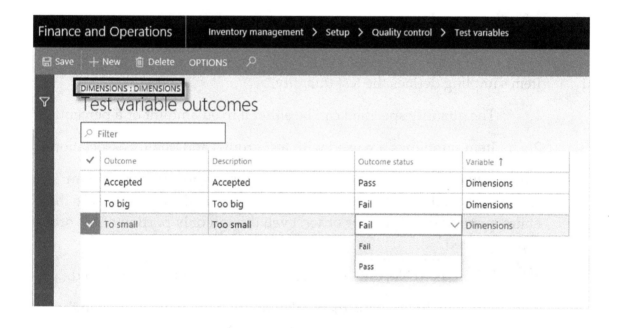

Item Sampling

Note: Instructions precede screen copies

1. Item sampling defines the test quantity.

    1. The quantity specified can be either a fixed amount or a percentage.

    2. Item samplings are used with test groups and quality associations.

2. Optionally use 'Full blocking' with item sampling to prevent the item from being used until the quality test is passed. Full blocking blocks the entire quantity of the item or order, even though only portion of the order is being tested.

    1. When set to No, only the quantity on the quality order is used.

    2. If the quality order is manually created, only the quantity on the quality order is used regardless of the full blocking setting.

3.   Optional, 'Per updated quantity' creates quality orders based on the actual physical quantity that is received.

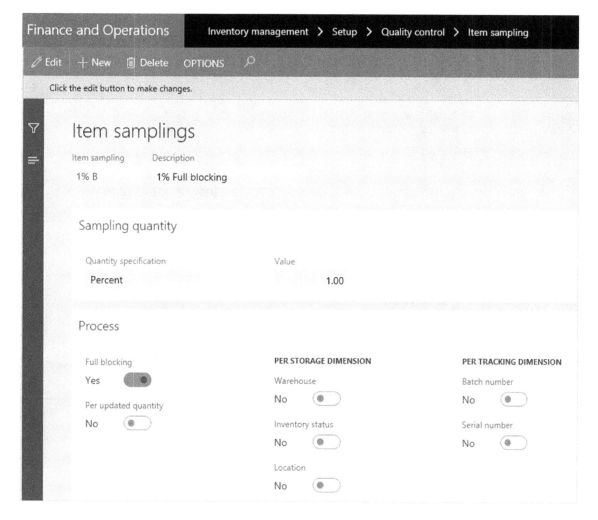

Test Groups

Note: Instructions precede screen copies

1. The upper pane displays test groups, and the lower pane displays the test(s) that are assigned to the selected test group.
2. UPPER – Group definition includes a sampling plan, an acceptable quality level (AQL), and if applicable a requirement for destructive testing.
3. LOWER – Test assignments include sequences, and if applicable, documents, and validity dates. Quantitative tests include acceptable measurement values. Qualitative tests include test variables and default outcomes.
4. The test group that is assigned to a quality order lists the tests that have to be performed on the specified item. Tests can be added, deleted, or changed on the quality order. Test results are reported for each test on a quality order.

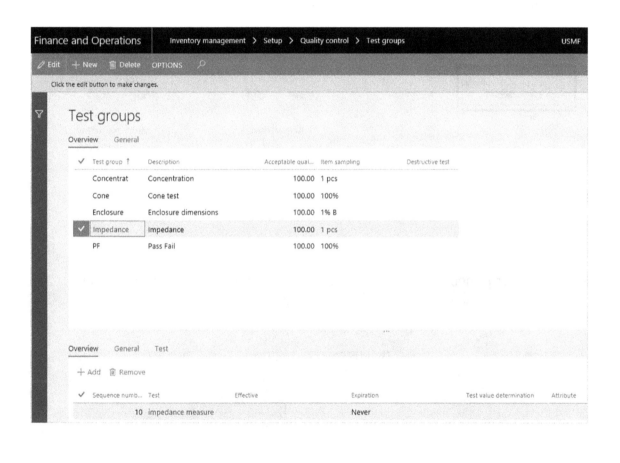

Finance and Operations   Inventory management > Setup > Quality control > Test groups   USMF

✎ Edit   + New   🗑 Delete   OPTIONS   🔎

Click the edit button to make changes.

Test groups

Overview   General

✓	Test group ↑	Description	Acceptable qual...	Item sampling	Destructive test
	Concentrat	Concentration	100.00	1 pcs	
	Cone	Cone test	100.00	100%	
	Enclosure	Enclosure dimensions	100.00	1% B	
✓	Impedance	Impedance	100.00	1 pcs	
	PF	Pass Fail	100.00	100%	

Overview   General   Test

+ Add   🗑 Remove

✓	Sequence numb...	Test	Effective	Expiration	Test value determination	Attribute
	10	impedance measure		Never		

5.   Lower panel, General tab, displays the editable <u>test</u>

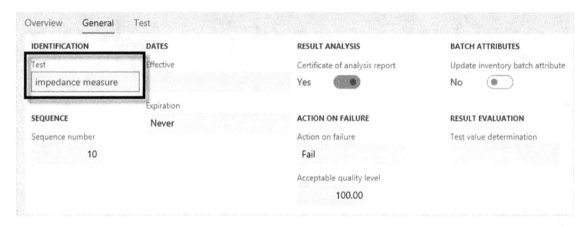

6.   Lower panel, Test tab sets the <u>test variable</u>: example set to Variable 'Impendence' with outcomes of pass/fail

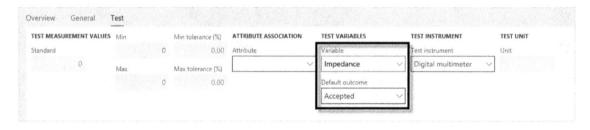

Quality Groups

Note: Instructions precede screen copies

1.   Items with common testing requirements can be assigned to a quality group. The quality group can then be assigned to the Quality Association.

    1.   The part is assigned to the group in Released Products, via the add item button on the form, or via Item Quality Groups.

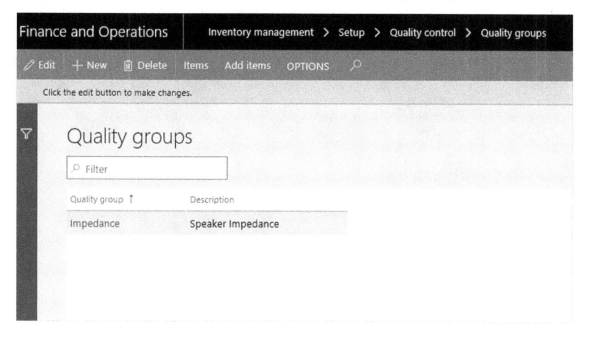

Item Quality Groups

Note: Instructions precede screen copies

1. Assign parts to Quality Groups

    1. Quality Group can then be assigned to a Quality Association to enable automatic generation of quality orders (see below)

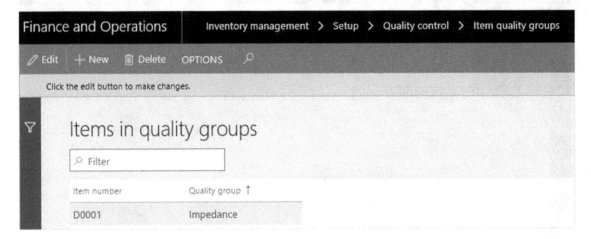

Quality Associations

Note: Instructions precede screen copies

1. Use this form to set up quality associations for **Quality Orders** on one or more items.

2. Quality orders can be generated for purchase orders, quarantine orders, sales orders, and production orders.

3. A quality association defines the following for a quality order:

    1. The transaction event

    2. The set of tests that must be performed on the item

    3. The acceptable quality level (AQL)

    4. The sampling plan

4. The Quality Association can be assigned to the **part (Table item code)** or **quality group (Group item code)**

    1. The Quality Group can also be applied to the part in Released Products or directly to the group. (see quality groups below)

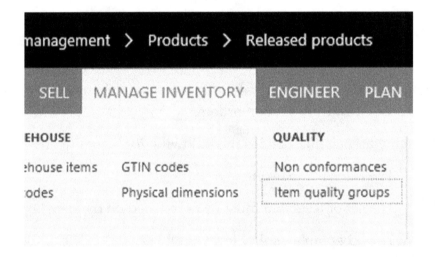

5.   Infolog notifications are enabled via the Show Info flag

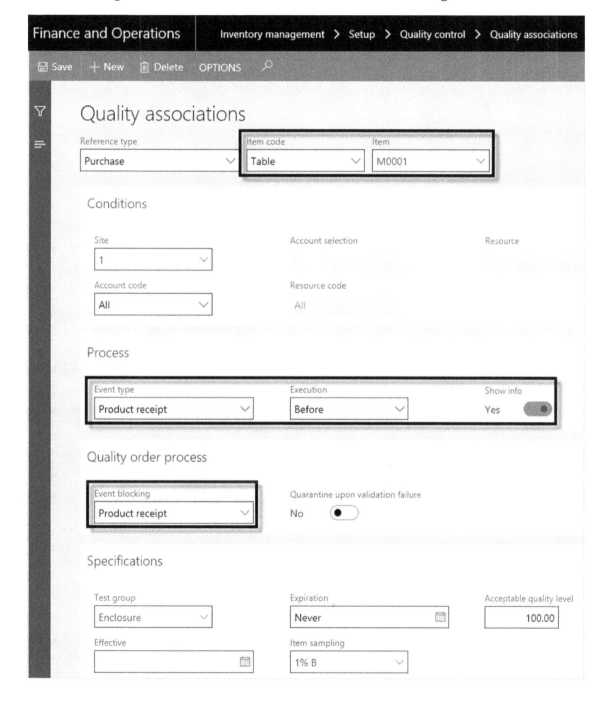

6. Reference types for quality order associations:
    1. Note that a quarantine order option is available

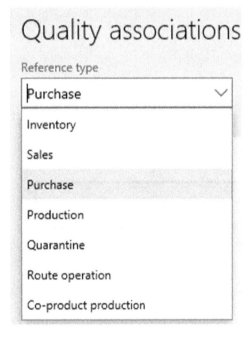

7.   Process and Quality Order Process fast tabs:
    1.   'Event type' pull down options, and 'Event blocking' pull down options **change with Reference Type**
    2.   Note that execution of blocking can be before or after the Event Type
    3.   Auto quarantine on validation failure is also available (flag is disabled for reference type quarantine)

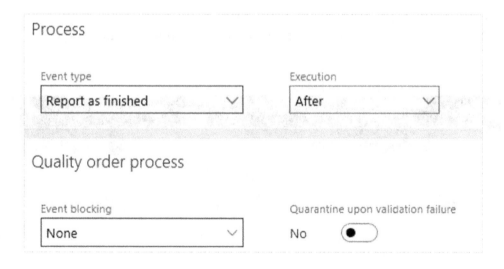

Workers Responsible for Quality

Note: Instructions precede screen copies

1.   Optional, assign worker(s) responsible for quality
     1.   Is used by Non-conformance
     2.   Can use the hourly rate setting established in inventory management parameters (see above)
     3.   Note that worker and worker responsible settings can be unique

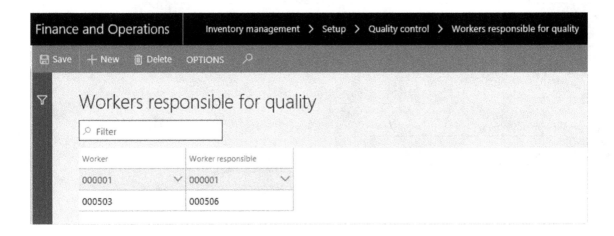

TRANSACTION EXAMPLES

Quarantine Order, Automatic

Note: Instructions precede screen copies

Production order example

1.   Using Contoso, Item Model Group STDQ has Quarantine Management enabled

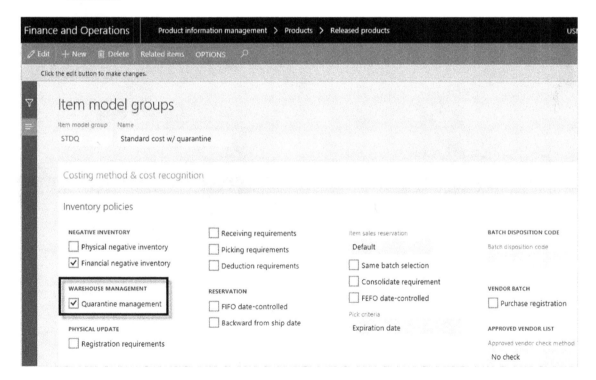

2. Part D0001 has been assigned Item Model group STDQ

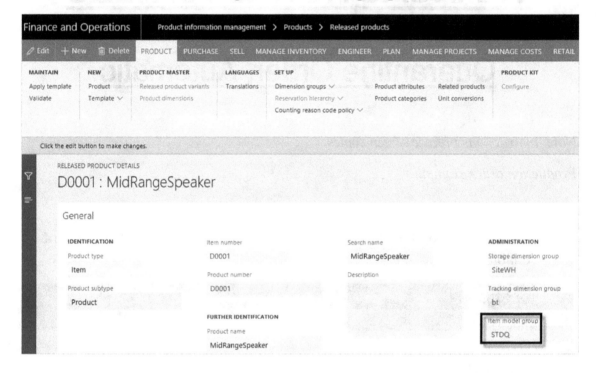

3. Production Order is RAF'd

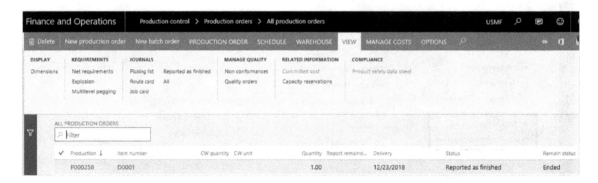

4. Quarantine Order is created
   1. Note status started

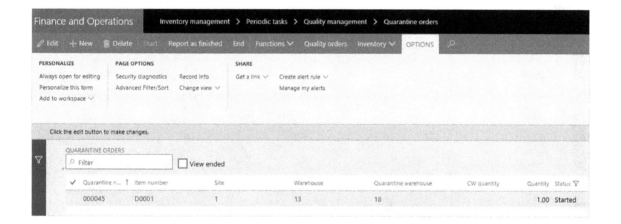

5.   Quarantine Order details, note reference to Production Order
   1.   Quality Order can now be optionally created from Quality Order
         button at top of form

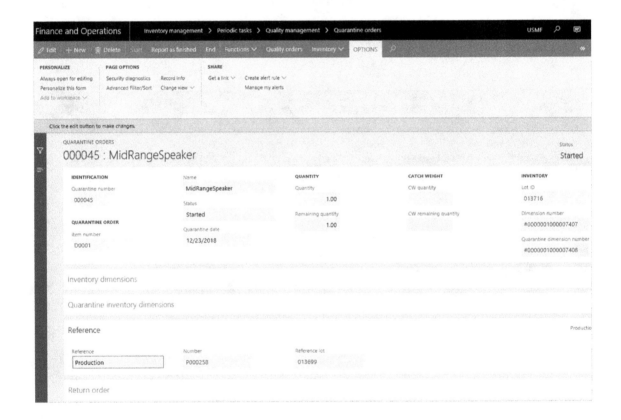

6. From Released Products Inventory action tab, note on hand inventory with reserved quarantined warehouse quantity

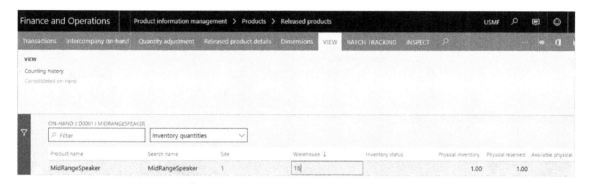

7. RAF and End Quarantine Order, note status Ended

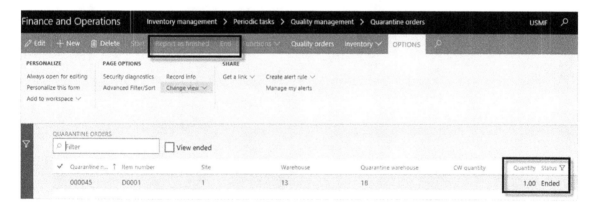

8.   From Released Products, note inventory has been released from the Quarantine Warehouse, and that warehouse 18 is no longer listed as an on hand location

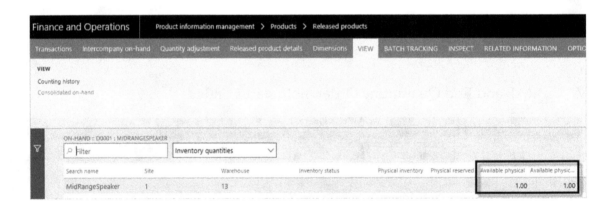

Quality Order, Manual (Prod Order)

Note: Instructions precede screen copies

Example will approve quality order

1.   Note: on hand inventory prior to quality order create
    1.   Physical reserved = 11

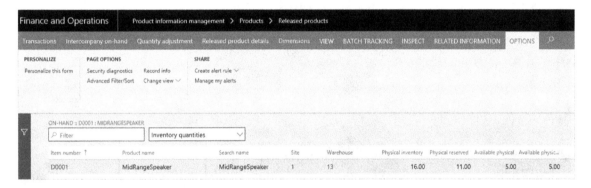

2.   Using production part that does not have a quality association assignment, RAF a production order.
    1.   Create a manual quality order from the View action tab > Manage Quality > Quality Orders

3. **Apply a Test Group**
4. **Update quantity if required**
   1. example is @ 1
5. **production order reference is defaulted**

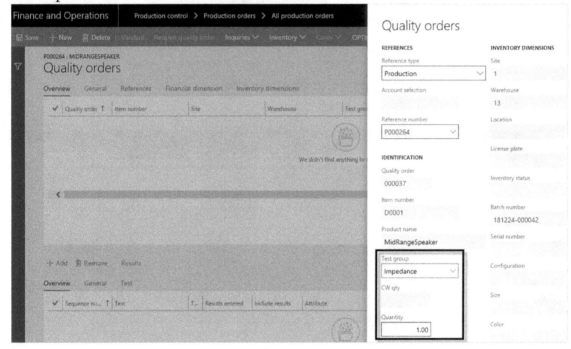

6. **Note: Reserved quantity has been increased by 1**

7.   In lower panel, add test(s)
    1.   Note Test and Test Variable are defaulted from the Test Group

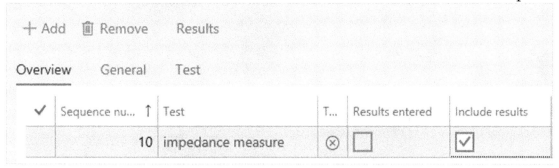

8.   On Test tab, update action to 'Accept', and Save

9. Note test result is updated to green check mark, Pass

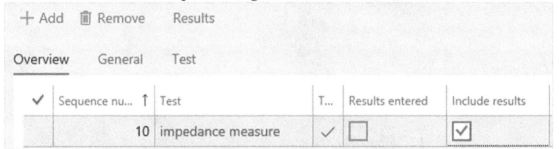

10. Validate Quality Order

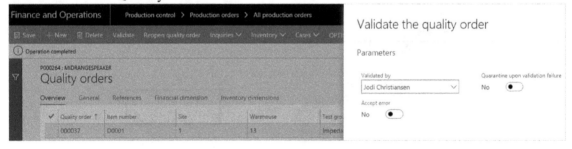

11. Note status update to Pass

12. Note on reserved has been reduced by 1

Quality Order, Automatic (Pur Order)

Note: Instructions precede screen copies

Example will fail 1 of 2 pcs

Auto Quality Order is created post PO receipt

From Quality Order, <u>Quarantine Order is manually created</u> @ 2 pcs

<u>1 pc is scrapped</u> from Quarantine

Balance of the quarantine is approved and released to inventory

1. Part M0001 Quality Association
    1. Blocking <u>after</u> product receipt
    2. Invoicing is the blocked event
    3. Sampling blocks full transaction quantity

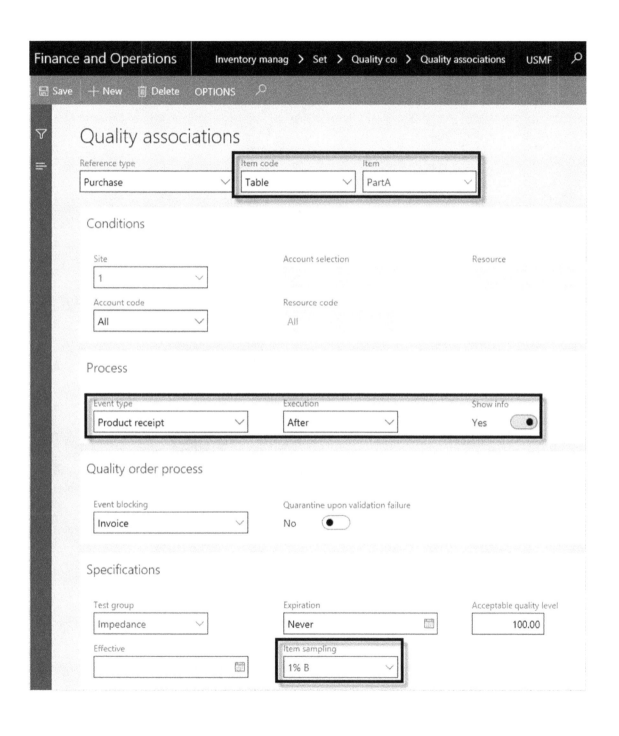

2. Item Samplings with full blocking set to yes

Item samplings

Item sampling | Description
1% B | 1% Full blocking

Sampling quantity

Quantity specification

Percent ⌄

Value

1.00

Process

Full blocking

Yes ●

Per updated quantity

No ●

Inventory status

No ●

Location

No ●

PER STORAGE DIMENSION

Warehouse

No ●

PER TRACKING DIMENSION

Batch number

No ●

Serial number

No ●

3. Note PartA On Hand and Ordered Reserve @ 0

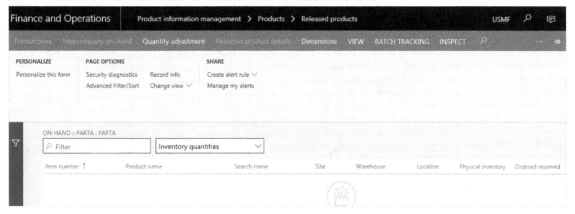

4. PO confirmed at 2 pcs

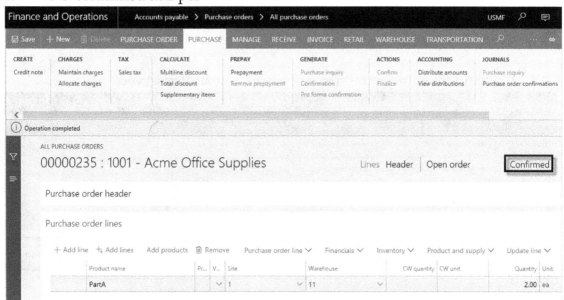

5.   PO receipt results in an auto quality order create

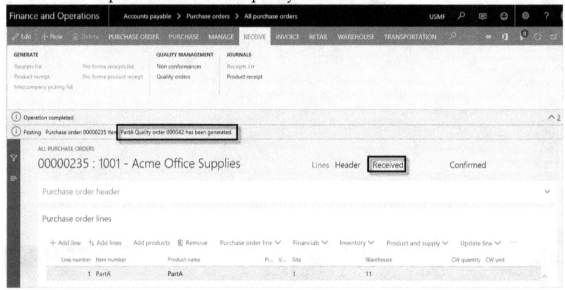

6.   On hand inventory now shows 2 pcs in 'physical reserved'

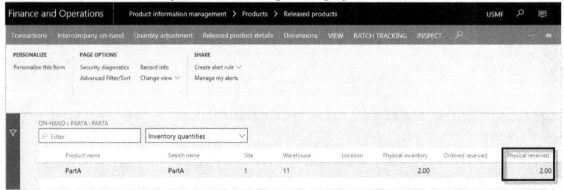

7.   Note test group item sampling tests at 1 pc

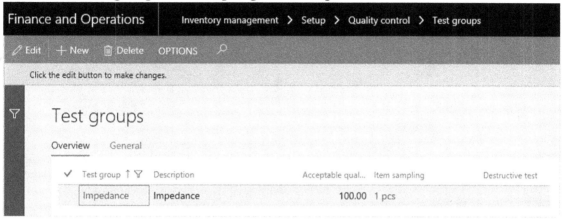

8.   Open Quality Order
    1.   Quantity = 1
    2.   Order is @ status Open
    3.   Test result shows 'red X'
9.   Highlight order and **click blue Results button** in lower panel

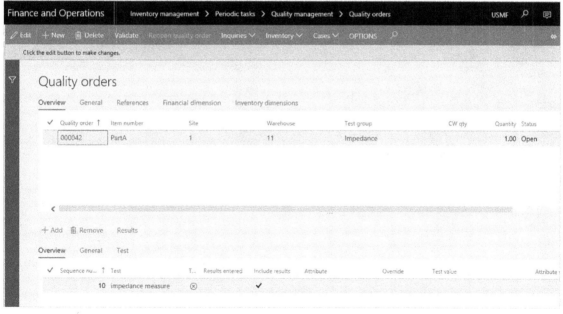

10.   Click Edit (note default outcome is at Accepted, and test result @ 'red X')

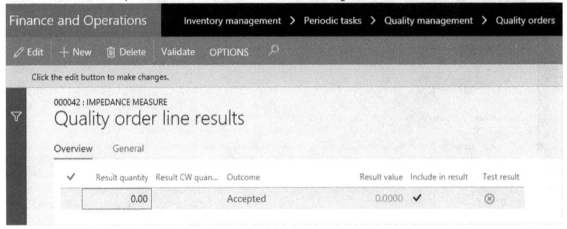

11.   Enter quantity and change outcome to Too Big (fail)
        1.   Validate the Test
        2.   Save
        3.   Close

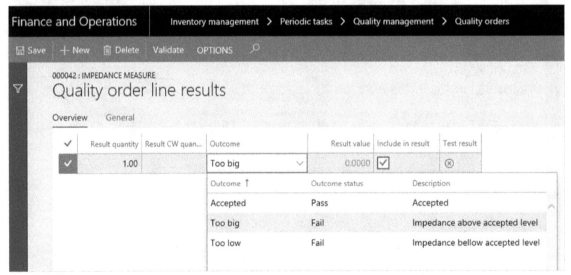

12. Highlight Quality Order and Validate
    1. Turn ON (Yes) Quarantine Upon Validation Failure
    2. Click OK

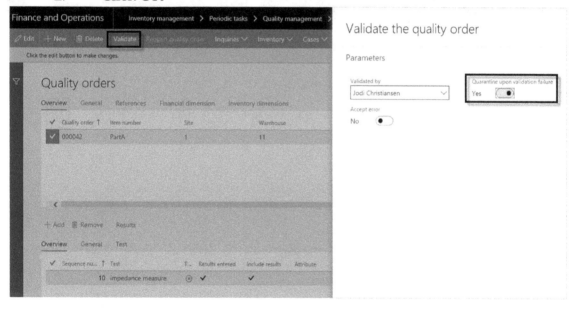

13.   Quality order changed to Fail

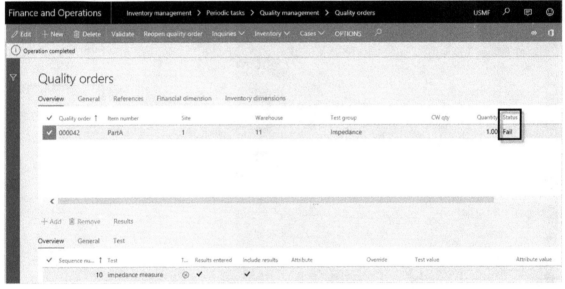

14. On Hand verifies product has been move to quarantine warehouse 18 and remains as physical reserved

   1. **Best practice recommendation**: The sequence of automatic quarantine to quality order, or its reverse, has to be considered carefully. In some instances this can result in critical stop or infolog messages. **Test your setup with a transaction that uses an initial 0 on hand quantity to verify the validity of your QC process.**

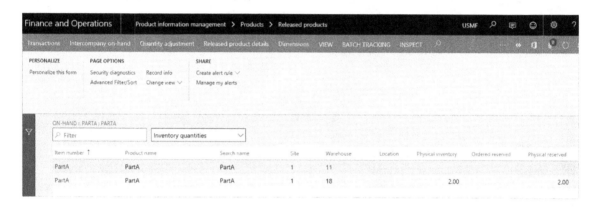

15. Open quarantine order
   1. Note quantity is equal to the full PO receipt

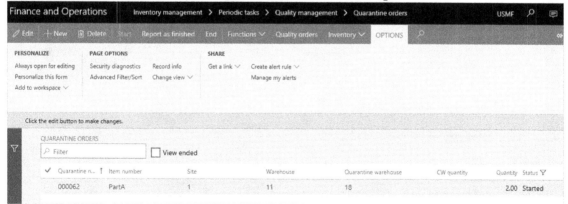

16. Open quarantine order detail
    1. Note PO reference
    2. and that both warehouse 11 and 18 are listed

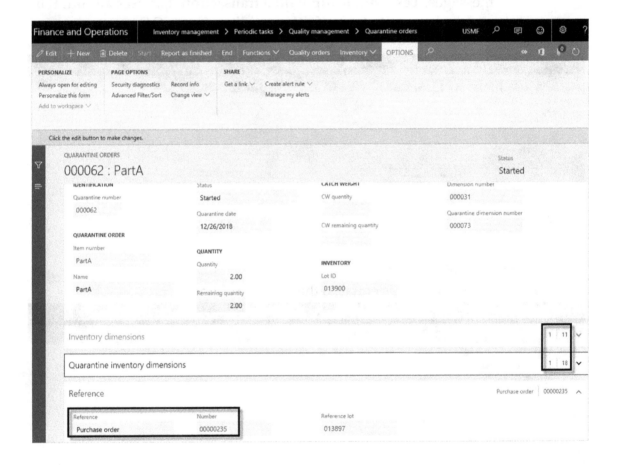

17.   From Functions pull down, select Scrap
1.   Quarantine Orders can also be split from the pull down

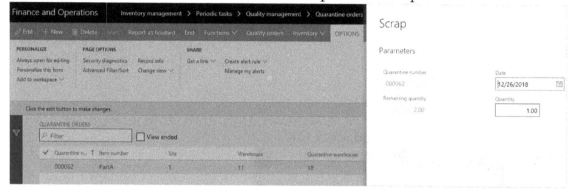

18.   Remaining Quantity now shows 1

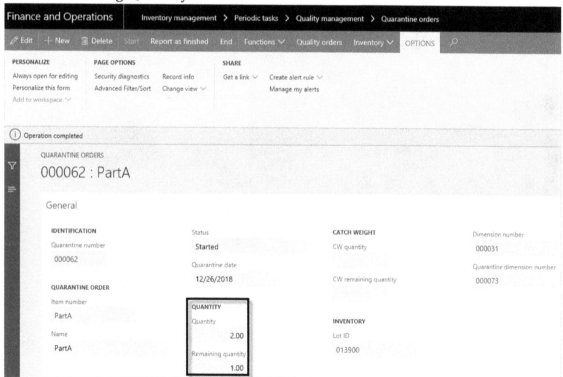

19.   Click Report as Finished, click OK

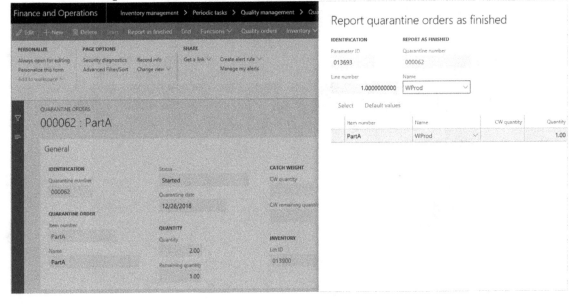

20. Click End, and click OK

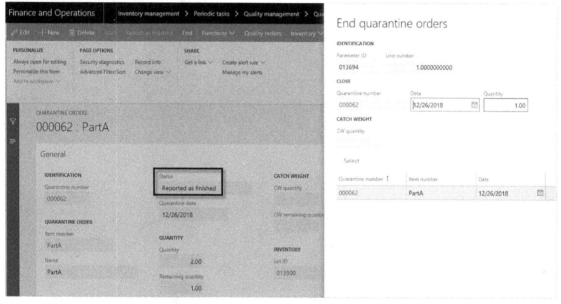

21. Status is @ Ended, remaining quantity = 0

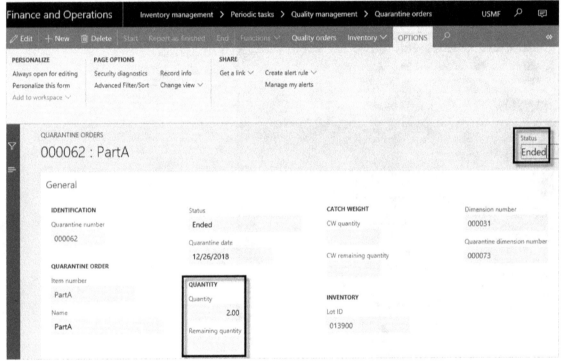

22.   Inventory updated to warehouse 11 @ 1 pc
       1.   Inventory has been decremented from warehouse 18
       2.   1 pc has been scrapped

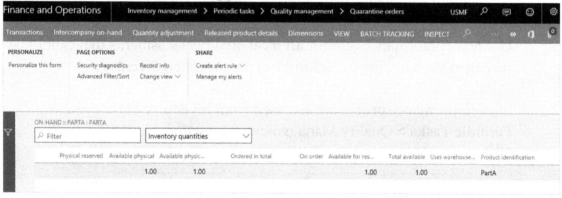

Non-Conformances

Note: Instructions precede screen copies

1. Non-conformances describe products and items that do not comply with predefined performance or quality standards.

2. Non-conformances apply to customer service or internal problems, such as customer complaints or production issues.

3. Use non-conformances are for atypical quality assessments that cannot be managed via a quality order, and has no impact on inventory

4. Non-conformance orders are accessed from Inventory Management > **Periodic Tasks** > Quality Management sub-section

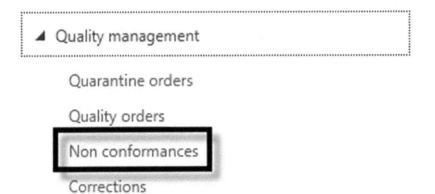

5. Access forms associated with non-conformance setup from the Inventory Management > **Setup** > Quality Management sub-section

   In order of suggested setup:

   1. Problem Types: Non-conformance cause
   2. > Diagnostic Types: Diagnostic actions
   3. > Operations: Processes used to correct or rework
   4. > Quality Miscellaneous Charges: User operation charges
   5. > Quarantine Zone: Tag items to prevent release

   ◢ Quality management

      Diagnostic types

      Quality charges

      Operations

      Problem types

      Quarantine zones

6.   Problem Types
    1.   Problem types that can be authorized for nonconformance types

Finance and Operations   Inventory management > Setup > Quality management > Problem types

Edit   + New   Delete   Non conformance types   OPTIONS

Click the edit button to make changes.

Problem types

Filter

Problem type ↑	Description
Deviating Impedance	Impedance outside of desired ra...
Enclosure	Wrong dimensions
pf	pf

    2.   Click Non Conformance Types to enter types that can be
          authorized for non-conformances

DEVIATING IMPEDANCE : IMPEDANCE OUTSIDE OF DESIRED RANGE

Problem/Non conformance types validation

Filter

✓	Non conformance type
	Vendor
	Internal

7.   Diagnostic Types
     1.   Diagnostic actions that will be used to process and correct non-
          conformances

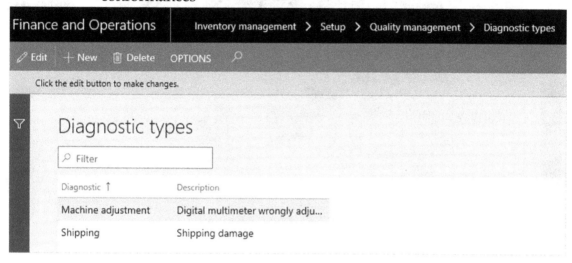

8.   Operations
     1.   Operations or activities that are used to process or resolve non-
          conformances

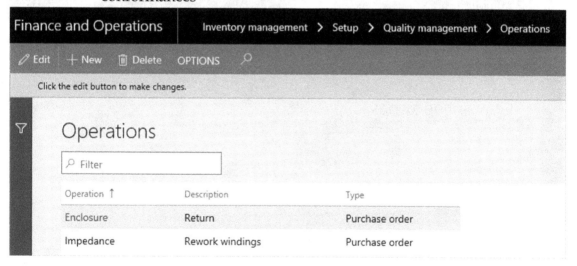

9. Quality Miscellaneous Charges
    1. Charges incurred when a user performs activities or operations that are related to a non-conformance

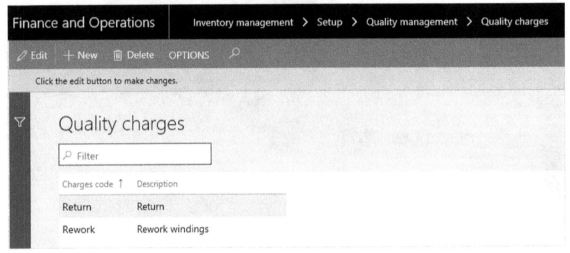

10. Quarantine Zone
    1. Used to highlight and tag items that do not meet conformance standards

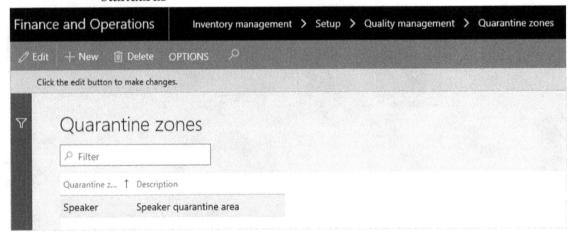

11. From Inventory Management > **Periodic Tasks**, open the non-conformances form, and click New. Select Type if applicable (example uses Internal)

    1. **Internal**: Quality-order number or a lot number of a quality-order transaction. For example, the nonconformance could relate to the tests that are performed as part of a quality order or to an employee's concern about product quality.

    2. **Customer**: Customer account number, sales order number, or a lot number of a sales order transaction. For example, the nonconformance could relate to customer feedback about product quality.

    3. **Vendor**: Vendor account number, purchase order number, or a lot number of a purchase order transaction. For example, the nonconformance could relate to a vendor's concern about a part that it supplies.

4. **Service request**: Customer account number, sales order number, or a lot number of a sales order transaction. For example, the nonconformance could relate to a customer's complaint about item quality.

5. **Production and Co-Product Production**: Production order number or a lot number of a production order transaction. For example, the nonconformance could relate to a specific batch that was produced.

Non conformance type

| Internal | ∨ |

Internal

Customer

Vendor

Service request

Production

Co-product production

12. Enter item, worker if applicable, problem type, and quantity
    1. and click OK
        1. Note quality workers are assigned via the workers responsible for quality form (see above)

13. Overview tab

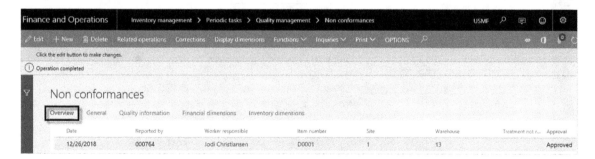

14. General tab
    1. Non-conformance has no impact on items in inventory.
    2. Quarantine zone is only used for reporting purposes, and is displayed on a nonconformance tag to guide the disposition of defective material.
    3. Quarantine type restricts usage or designates the product as unusable.
    4. The quarantine type is displayed on a nonconformance tag to guide the disposition of defective material.

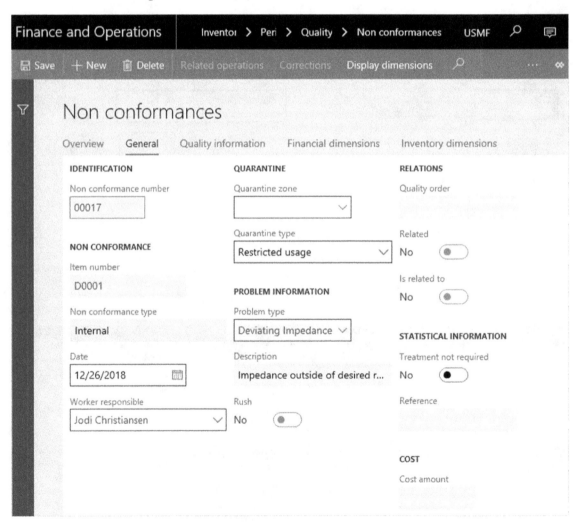

15. Related Items (Pull downs are enabled on **Approve**)
    1. Or non-conformance can be '**Refused**'
    2. When done both options can be '**Closed**'

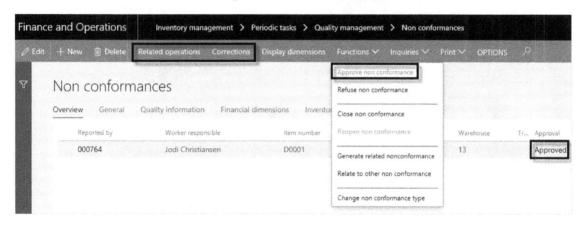

16. Enter operation, reason, and SO/PO if applicable
    1. <u>Save</u> enables pull downs

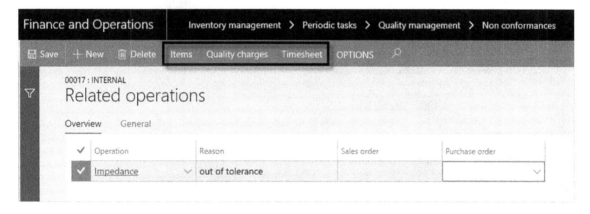

17.   Related operations (Items) – Use this form to reference a related Item that will be worked on in relation to the non-conformance defined part.

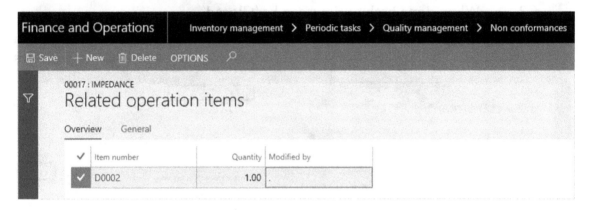

18.   Related operations (Quality charges) – Use this form to add additional quality charges that were required to apply the repair. These charges are accumulated at the non-conformance level and can be invoiced if appropriate.

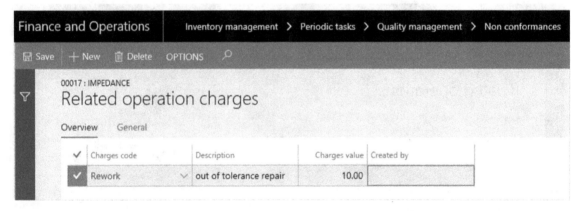

19. Related operations (Timesheet) – Use this form to report the work performed by the worker assigned. The hours entered will be multiplied by hourly rate specified in QM fast tab of the Inventory management parameters form, and are accumulated at the non-conformance level.

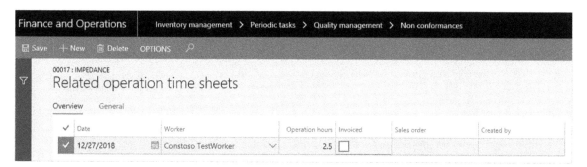

20. Corrections – Use this form to add corrections for non-conformance records
    1. Button is enabled via Approve

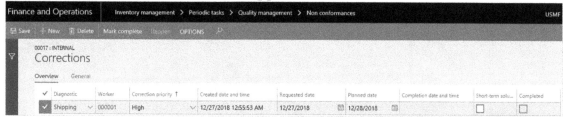

21. Mark complete to close

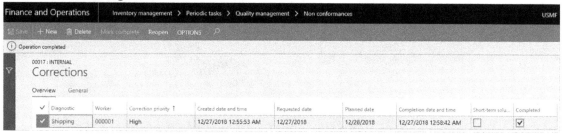

END

NOTES

www.ingramcontent.com/pod-product-compliance
Lightning Source LLC
Chambersburg PA
CBHW060205060326
40690CB00018B/4255